P9-DEI-097

Take the road to creativity and get off your dead end

By David Campbell, Ph.D.

Center for Creative Leadership
P. O. Box P-1
Greensboro, North Carolina 27402
U.S.A.

Acknowledgments

Excerpt from "The Discovery of the J Particle: A Personal Recollection" by Samuel C. C. Ting. Copyright © The Nobel Foundation 1977. Reprinted by permission.

Excerpt from "The Making of a Poem" by Stephen Spender. Copyright © 1946 by Stephen Spender. Renewal © 1974 by Stephen Spender. Reprinted by permission of Harold Matson Company, Inc.

Excerpt from "Mathematical Creation" by Henri Poincare. Translated by George Bruce Halsted. Copyright © 1943 by George Bruce Halsted. Reprinted from The Creative Process: A Symposium, edited by Brewster Ghiselin, The Univ. of California Press, 1952. By permission.

Excerpt from Creativity and Psychological Health by Frank Barron. New York, D. Van Nostrand Company, Inc., 1963. By permission.

Book review by Beverly Gary Kempton, Playboy Magazine, Volume 23, Number 12. Copyright © 1976. Reprinted by permission.

Excerpt from Present Indicative by Noel Coward. Copyright © 1937 by Noel Coward. Reprinted by permission of Doubleday & Company, Inc.

Excerpt from "The Relation of the Poet to Day-Dreaming," Volume 4, paper 9 in The Collected Papers of Sigmund Freud, edited by Ernest Jones, M.D., authorized translation under the supervision of Joan Riviere, published by Basic Books, Inc., Publishers, New York, by arrangement with The Hogarth Press, Ltd. and the Institute of Psycho-Analysis, London.

Sigmund Freud Copyrights Ltd., The Institute of Psycho-Analysis and The Hogarth Press Ltd. for permission to quote from "Creative Writers and Day-Dreaming" contained in Volume IX of The Standard Edition of the Complete Psychological Works of Sigmund Freud, translated and edited by James Strachey.

Excerpt from Bring on the Empty Horses by David Niven. Copyright © 1975 by David Niven. Reprinted by permission of the author's agent, International Creative Management.

Excerpt from Creativity and Personal Freedom by Frank Barron. New York, D. Van Nostrand Company, Inc., 1968. By permission.

Excerpt from "Edison as Record Producer" by Bridget Paolucci. Reprinted by permission of High Fidelity Magazine, January, 1977, Volume 27 Number 1. All rights reserved.

Excerpt from Creativity: Its Educational Implications, John Curtis Gowan, George D. Demos, E. Paul Torrance, editors. Copyright © 1967 by John Wiley & Sons, Inc. Reprinted by permission of John Wiley & Sons, Inc.

Excerpt from Portrait of Myself by Margaret Bourke-White. Copyright © 1963 by Margaret Bourke-White. Reprinted by permission of Simon and Schuster, Inc. and Collins Publishers, London.

Excerpt from On Being Funny: Woody Allen and Comedy by Eric Lax. Copyright © 1975 by Eric Lax. Reprinted by permission of David McKay Co., Inc.

Excerpt from "Stress: On Mount Everest" by James T. Lester. Reprinted from Psychology Today Magazine, September 1969, Volume 3, Number 4. Copyright © 1969 Ziff-Davis Publishing Company.

Excerpt from The Money Game by "Adam Smith." Copyright © 1967, 1968 by Adam Smith. Reprinted by permission of Random House, Inc.

Excerpt from "Gregory Peck in MacArthur: An Old Soldier Returns Again" by Joseph N. Bell. The National Observer, May 30, 1977. Reprinted with permission of The National Observer, copyright © Dow Jones Co., Inc, (1977). All rights reserved.

Specified abridged adaptation of material from pp. 14-15 of Self-Renewal: The Individual and the Innovative Society by John W. Gardner. Copyright © 1963, 1964 by John W. Gardner. Reprinted by permission of Harper & Row Publishers, Inc.

Cover Design by Gene Tarpey
Illustrations by Nicole Hollander

FIRST EDITION

© Copyright 1985 David P. Campbell

All rights reserved. No portion of this book may be reproduced, stored in a retrieval system, or transmitted in any form by any means—electronic, mechanical, photocopying, recording, or otherwise—without prior permission of the copyright owner.

Printed in the United States of America.

Center for Creative Leadership
P. O. Box P-1
Greensboro, North Carolina 27402
U.S.A.

International Standard Book Number: 0-912879-91-2
Library of Congress Number: 77-92128

9 8 7 6 5 4 3 2 1

Contents

"There's no use trying," said Alice. "One *can't* believe impossible things."

"I daresay you haven't had much practice," said the Queen. "When I was your age, I always did it for half-an-hour a day. Why, sometimes I've believed as many as six impossible things before breakfast."

. . . Lewis Carroll
Through the Looking-Glass

Introduction

Bringing something new into existence is one of life's most exquisite joys; whether it is a new machine, a new idea, a new recipe, a new song, a new person, a new garden, or a new political program, our creation has our own stamp on it, and the parental pride is almost intoxicating.

We all can do it; everyone has powers of imagination and creative talent. In some people, these are highly developed and we can see the results in the works of great artists, writers, architects, inventors, and scientists. In other cases—probably the majority—these creative qualities lie dormant and untapped.

Where to begin?. . . Wherever you are. As Teddy Roosevelt said, "Do what you can, with what you have, where you are." But inevitably there is going to be some startup static. Psychologists who have studied creative products have noticed that new things frequently appear only after a period of heavy concentration and, perhaps, frustration. Only after the searcher has

apparently hit a dead end does the breakthrough come, usually from energetically starting off in a new direction. Consequently, in more ways than one, if you want to create something new, you have to start by getting off your dead end.

The results are worth it.

After all, if you are living a humdrum life and do nothing to change it, ten years from now you will be the product of ten more years of humdrumedness.

There are, of course, more important arguments in favor of creativity—we desperately need innovative thinkers to solve the problems of war, greed, pestilence, famine, and loneliness. . . . Still, at the personal level, the individual creator is usually more interested in sweeping back the waves of boredom than in eliminating wars, pestilence, and greed.

In my more irreverent moments, I suspect that the major reason God created Heaven and Earth was to have something interesting to do.

Creativity demands commitment. To change one's life even in small ways requires energy, participation, and enthusiasm. You cannot be creative while inert. You have to get involved. In reading this book expect to participate. Take out a pencil and try the exercises as they are presented. If you are unable to actually write down your answers, work them through mentally before going on.

Take One
Wheelbarrow

Below is a side view of a proposed design for a
new wheelbarrow. Write down five comments
about this design.

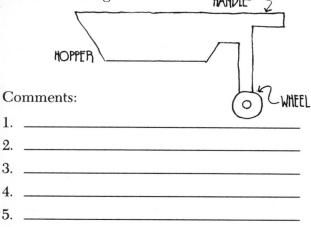

Comments:

1. _____

2. _____

3. _____

4. _____

5. _____

Come on now! Don't read ahead without thinking up comments on this wheelbarrow!!

Look over your comments—do you see any general theme? In particular, are they all critical? If you are like most people, your comments look something like this:

1. *The wheel is too small.*

2. *The handle is too short.*

3. *It's poorly balanced.*

4. *It won't hold much.*

5. *Some version of "stupid," "ridiculous," or "ha ha ha ha!"...*

Yet, if you will look back at my instructions, you will see that I asked you to *comment* on my wheelbarrow, not to pick on it. Why do you feel such a compulsion to criticize?!!

You are not alone; virtually everyone, when asked to comment on this wheelbarrow, focuses on the flaws. Why? What is this general tendency to degrade new ideas? Surely there is at least *something* good that can be said about this wheelbarrow—or at least something neutral.

And there is. Children who are shown this design—kids around 10-12 who haven't yet acquired the adult propensity for constant fault-finding with new ideas—say the following kinds of things:

Comment: "That's a very interesting wheel-barrow. Because the handle is so short, if you got some mud on the wheel, you could reach right over and kick it off."

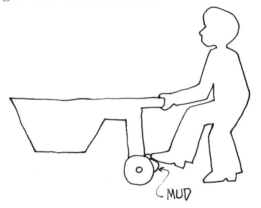

Comment: "Hey, that's a neat wheelbarrow—you could wheel that right up to the edge of a hole and empty it over the edge."

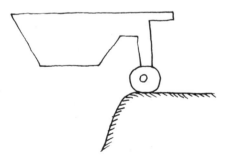

Comment: "Yeah, and that design gives you the opportunity to put a little trapdoor in the bottom of the hopper and empty it easily by just pulling on a string."

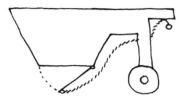

Comment: (This is my favorite) "Wow, that's a great design because it allows you to build in a simple way to tell if the wheelbarrow is overloaded. You could put a piston inside the wheel support with a spring on the top. Then cut a little window in the support through which you can see the piston. You paint half the piston red, half green. When you have too much weight in the barrow, the red shows and you know you are carrying too much."

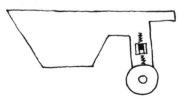

HOW GOOD IS AN IDEA?

Professor Edward de Bono of Cambridge University, who taught me this wheelbarrow gimmick and who collected these solutions from children, has an important explanation for the unusual creativity of these children. Before they worked on the problem, he taught them a special approach to new ideas, using the acronym, PNI: P for *positive*, N for *negative*, and I for *interesting*. "When you meet with a new idea," says de Bono, "ask yourself at least three questions: First, what are the positives of this idea? Second, what are the negatives? and third—and FAR MORE IMPORTANT—what are the interesting things about this idea? Don't feel the need to either support or criticize the new

13

idea—just sit there and ponder . . . 'Hmmm . . . that's an interesting idea that I have never thought about before. What can I do with it?'" That is the orientation that the 12-year-olds had when they came to the wheelbarrow; they weren't looking for good or bad points—they were looking for interesting points. Obviously, their comments would be more helpful in designing a radically new kind of wheelbarrow than the kind of criticisms that most people (including you?) come up with.

Interesting reactions are more creative than *critical* ones.

Further, I can guarantee you that criticisms are easy to come by. You needn't worry about overlooking them. Show that wheelbarrow to anyone, and you will get a flurry of criticisms. You don't need to worry about missing the flaws; lots of people will point them out to you. But if you want to create something radically new, you have to see the interesting potential yourself; you cannot count on others for that, unless of course you can introduce them to the PNI way of thinking also.

Here are some examples of interesting reactions to everyday problems and situations. The ideas are all creative even though incomplete and far-out.

The tabs from poptop cans are a nuisance; they create litter. How about a law that says that the tabs have to be made of dimes, so that every time you open a can of beer or soda, you can put ten cents in your pocket?

Why not build a tape recorder into a refrigerator so that every time the door is opened, a recorded message plays. . . . It may be a diet control message—"STOP! EATING THOSE CALORIES WILL MAKE YOU FAT AND SLOPPY. YOU ARE WHAT YOU EAT." . . . or a commercial—"WHILE YOU ARE IN THE REFRIGERATOR, HOW ABOUT TRYING A FRESH SLIVER OF DELICIOUS COUNTRY HAM?"

Why not have retractable billboards that could be withdrawn on Sundays and holidays so that people could enjoy pleasant weekend drives with no distractions?

These ideas are far from perfect in their current form, but where else might they lead us?

They are good examples of ideas which can be approached through the PNI way of thinking. What's good about the idea ? What are its flaws? Does the good outweigh the flaws?

WHAT I LIKE ABOUT THAT IS. . . .

One way to demonstrate why new ideas should not be immediately rejected because of obvious flaws is "The Idea Spectrum," a concept developed by researchers at Synectics, Inc., a Boston creativity-training firm. This technique locates new ideas along a scale that runs from *worthless* to *perfection*. Each idea's location on the spectrum is determined by the

ratio of pluses and minuses that the idea has. A new idea with no positive features whatsoever, and they are rare, is worthless; a new idea without a single negative, which is even rarer, is perfection. Most new ideas fall somewhere between the extremes; like people, they are almost never completely good or bad; each has some assets, some liabilities.

Graphically, the Idea Spectrum looks like this:

```
- - + - - - - + - + - + + + - - + - + + + + + +
- - - - - - + - - - - - - + - + - + + - + + + +
- - - - - + - - - - + + + - + + - + + - + + + +
- + - - - - - - + - + - + - + - + + + + + - + +
- - - + - - + - + - + - + - + + + + - + + - + +
- - - + - - - - + - - + - + - + - + + - + + + +
- - - - - - + - + + + - + + + - + + + + + + + +
- - - - - + - - - - - - + + + - + + + + + + + +
- - - + - - + - + - + - + - + + + + + + + + + +
- - - - - - - - - + - - + - - + - + + + + + + +
```
                              ▲
                            THE
WORTHLESS   **ACCEPTABLE**   PERFECTION
                            LINE

Ideas with many good points fall above the Acceptable Line and can be adopted immediately. They may need some tinkering to solve, overcome, or eliminate a few negative features, but if the number of pluses is high enough, the idea can work right away.

Ideas that fall below the Acceptable Line are usually rejected because they have too many minuses ("The wheelbarrow handle is too short" or "The wheel is too small"); still, they do have some pluses ("It would be easy to empty"), and those pluses might be worth teasing out and saving. When the total idea is discarded because

17

of too many bad features, the fewer good features are also discarded and probably lost forever.

Some ideas, even those below the Acceptable Line, can often be saved. The trick is to nourish, modify, and nudge the new idea along the Idea Line by sifting out and saving the positive features while working on the negatives until they are eliminated. The idea then crosses the line into acceptability on its quest for perfection.

All you have to do to move a new idea into the Acceptable category is cluster together a large number of positive elements, at the same time eliminating the negative ones. That is what creativity—even life itself—is all about.

With this idea that *all* new ideas have some positive features—let's plunge ahead.

The Nature of Creativity

DEFINITION

Creativity is an action producing a result that is:

1. **Novel:** new, strange, innovative, "creative"— something that has not been seen before.

2. **Useful:** effective, solves a problem, helps, enchants, educates, persuades, entertains, or stimulates people—something that enriches and makes a change in someone's life.

3. **Understandable:** Other results like it can be produced in the future. Random events— unpredictable, unrepeatable—may be novel and useful, but they are the result of luck, not creativity. The one monkey out of 16 million trillion zillion monkeys sitting at typewriters who finally produces a Shakespeare sonnet is no more creative than the person who throws

16 million trillion zillion pennies in the air and watches them all come down heads. Both are rare events, but neither is creative—both are pure luck.

CREATIVITY CLOSE-UP

A creative act means a change in direction. But how is this done? The following illustration helps to explain how new ideas emerge to change a situation or solve a problem. I first saw this in a lecture given by Professor de Bono; because his ideas about the creative process

are so close to my own, I have enthusiastically adopted many of them.

The Search represents a pathway that we are on, seeking a solution to a problem. "THE DEAD END" is where we will end up if we go on as usual; when creativity is required, the solution almost certainly does not lie straight ahead of us. If it did, we would only have to do more of whatever we are now doing, and we would succeed. But a new idea is needed—one that will get us off the usual routine. Otherwise we will plow blindly ahead into the DEAD END.

The Creative Solution, represented by the path in the upper right-hand corner, is the new idea, the improved technique that sets us off in a new direction. In this illustration, the solution

21

is located in a particular place, but that is for example only; it could be anywhere in the jungle surrounding "THE SEARCH." When you are searching for a creative solution, you don't know where it is—except that it isn't straight ahead.

The Lucky Porthole is the little opening in the SEARCH path leading directly to the solution. If you are lucky enough to find this porthole (by intuition, hunch) you can easily see the new direction. Through "luck," you avoid the jungle, reach the new solution and wonder why other people could not see the answer as easily as you did. And, looking backwards, whether you came through the lucky porthole shortcut or struggled tortuously through the jungle, the solution seems obvious, and the problem, simple.

FEATURES OF THE CREATIVE PROCESS

Although this is a simple diagram, it illustrates several features of the creative process:

1. **The pressure to continue straight ahead,** unchanging, with whatever you are currently doing.

2. **The ultimate dead end ahead,** "If you don't change directions, you will wind up where you are heading."

3. **The tortuous route** one usually has to follow in reaching a creative solution. There are no beaten pathways, no guideposts, no navigational aids. If there were, the solution would be common, not creative. If you want to be creative, you must expect occasionally to feel lost—but not much more often than occasionally. If you are lost all of the time, you are in the wrong jungle.

4. **The occasional "lucky" short cut** for finding the best solution. The answer itself is not accidental; sometimes it is the only possible one. What is accidental is the way that it is discovered.

5. **The necessary change of direction** to find the new solution. Creative solutions will always be off in some unexpected direction.

6. **The surprising simplicity of the solution,** looking backwards. Hindsight is all-powerful. A great philosopher once pointed out that the main difficulty in life is that although we can understand it backwards, we have to live it forwards.

AN EXERCISE

Let me show you a simple exercise to demonstrate these features. Following is a series of addition problems. The first has two numbers to be added together; the second adds in a third number; the next adds in a fourth number, and so forth. Each problem contains one more number to be added to the sum from the preceding one.

Write down each answer as you go; if you are where you can talk, also say the answer aloud.

```
        1000
          40
```
Total =

Remember,
say the answer aloud.

```
        1000
          40
        1000
```
Total =

```
        1000
          40
        1000
          30
```
Total =

```
        1000
          40
        1000
          30
        1000
```
Total =

```
                    1000
                      40
                    1000
                      30
                    1000
                      20
Total =
```

```
                    1000
                      40
                    1000
                      30
                    1000
                      20
                    1000
Total =
```

```
                    1000
                      40
                    1000
                      30
                    1000
                      20
                    1000
                      10
Total =
```

What answer did you finally come up with? If you wrote down 5000, you are like most people, and you are wrong. The correct answer is 4100. Go back and check your addition to see where you went astray.

This is a trivial example, but it does neatly demonstrate the principle; many times we rush headlong down a pathway that takes us quickly to where we don't want to go. Because the pattern in these problems lulls us into the rhythm of "one thousand, two thousand, three thousand, four thousand," five thousand seems so natural that we can't help ourselves. Yet the correct answer lies somewhere else, not in the learned pattern. Once we see it, in hindsight, it looks simple.

To demonstrate the process to your friends and, if you wrote down the correct answer, to show you how few people come up with the right answer, write down the numbers on a card like this:

$$
\begin{array}{r}
1000 \\
40 \\
1000 \\
30 \\
1000 \\
20 \\
1000 \\
\underline{10} \\
4100
\end{array}
$$

Now use a second piece of paper, cover everything but the top two numbers, show them to some friends and ask them to add the two numbers together, out loud, in unison. When they reply, "One thousand forty," slide the paper down one line exposing the next number, ask them to add in the next number, and they will answer, "Two thousand forty."

Keep sliding the paper down, uncovering the numbers one by one, until you reach the last one, when they will respond, "Five thousand." You can then use the opportunity to explain to them the nature of creativity.

HOW LUCKY CAN YOU GET?

Anyone who studies the creative process occasionally notices the presence of chance— "luck." Indeed, to the outsider, new creations sometimes appear to be almost entirely accidental. The runaway economic success of the Pet Rock during the 1975 Christmas season is a good example: Gary Dahl designed a box, put a plain rock in it, wrote a few clever words of instruction ("Your PET ROCK will be a devoted friend and companion for many years to come. Rocks enjoy a rather long life span so the two of you will never have to part—at least not on your PET ROCK's account"), and sold hundreds of thousands.

27

Many of us thought, "Why didn't I think of that? . . . That's so simple. . . . The guy was lucky. . . . He just happened to come up with the right idea at the right time."

Creative people—inventors, writers, scientists, artists—are not so impressed by the power of luck. Typically they point out that, at least in their area, the luckiest people are those who work the hardest.

While luck may play a role, those who "chance" onto creative solutions are usually actively hunting a solution and are alert to anything that might turn up along the trail. Prepared people on the move are luckier than ignorant people at rest, a situation well illustrated by one of John D. Rockefeller's sisters when she said, "When it's raining porridge, you'll always find John's bowl right side up."

One final point: you can be as lucky and pre-pared as you want, but if you don't seize the chance when you see it, if you don't act, it may all come to naught. If you wish to take advantage of luck, figure out where it might rain porridge, get there early with the biggest bowl you can find, and keep it right side up.

The Phases
of Creativity

Creative people frequently report that in coming up with a new idea or product, they went through several phases, usually in the following order:

1. **Preparation**—Laying the groundwork. Learning the background of a situation.

2. **Concentration**—Being totally absorbed in the specific problem.

3. **Incubation**—Taking time out, a rest period. Seeking distractions.

4. **Illumination** (AHA!)—Getting the answer, the idea! The lightbulb goes on.

5. **Verification/Production**—Confronting and solving the practical problems. Other people are persuaded and enlisted. The work gets done.

PHASE ONE—PREPARATION

I will present a brief account of my work during the last 10 years leading to the discovery of a new family of elementary particles. . .

After many years of work, we have learned how to handle a high-intensity beam of $\sim 10^{11}$ γ-rays per second with a 2 to 3 percent duty cycle, at the same time using a detector that has a large mass acceptance, a good mass resolution of $\Delta M \approx 5$ Mev, and the ability to distinguish $\pi\pi$ from e^+e^- by a factor of $\geq 10^8$.

We can now ask a simple question: How many heavy photons exist? and what are their properties?

"The Discovery of the J Particle: A Personal Recollection" By Samuel C. C Ting, professor of physics, MIT, Nobel Prize winner.

While not all experts are creative, most creators are experts. You are not likely to invent a new artificial heart valve until you have spent many years studying the mechanics of valves, the details of fluid flow, and the anatomy of the heart. You are not likely to design radical new skyscrapers until you have a firm grounding in architectural design, principles of engineering, and the economic realities surrounding large construction projects.

32

Brilliant breakthroughs are almost always achieved by people who have spent several years preparing themselves.

Much of this groundwork has to be done on faith, or because it is interesting in itself, not as training for a specific project. Few of us can predict what problems we will be working on ten years from now, or even what problems we *want* to be working on ten years from now. Yet today's activities, especially learning experiences, will be our available background for solving unknown future problems. "Invention is little more than new combinations of those images which have been previously gathered and deposited in the memory. Nothing can be made of nothing; those who have laid up no material can produce no combinations."—Sir Joshua Reynolds.

PHASE TWO—CONCENTRATION

The problem of creative writing is essentially one of concentration, and the supposed eccentricities of poets are usually due to mechanical habits or rituals developed in order to concentrate. Concentration . . . is a focusing of the attention in a special way, so that the poet is aware of all the implications . . . of his idea, just as one might say that a plant was not concentrating on developing mechanically in one direction, but in many directions, towards the warmth and light with its leaves, and toward the water with its roots, all at the same time.

Stephen Spender, poet

Creative people are usually intense about what they are doing. Scientists, architects, artists, advertising people, writers, researchers, photographers, and innovative businessmen frequently report long periods of concentration on the problems they are trying to solve.

The person wears a filter that screens out other demands; work is shunted aside, families are ignored, social life is eliminated, daily schedules are meaningless.

An inventor developing a new closing device sees the world as populated only with things that close—zippers, buttons, door locks, car windows, elevator doors, screen latches. The

HOW CAN
I CREATE,
WHEN I AM
CONSTANTLY
INTERUPTED...

question, "How many ways can you close up something?" is an obsession. How do books close? How do tire valves trap in air? How do canal locks keep water out? How do mouse traps snap shut? A creative inventor will continually be searching for other meanings of "close" to broaden the possible solutions: "He has a closed mind." "The corporation closed its books for the year." "The country has a closed-door policy."

The concentration stage continues the learning of the preparation stage, but more intensely. It is a focusing time, a time of specific trial and error, of drawing together relevant materials, of false starts and failure. If success doesn't come within a reasonable time, the concentration takes on obsessive qualities. The inventor becomes frustrated, impatient! "Why can't I see the answer? It must be here somewhere."

PHASE THREE—INCUBATION

> I continued to go to the Bibliotheque Nationale; it is pleasant and restful to fill one's eyes with words that already exist, instead of having to wrest sentences from the void.
>
> Simone de Beauvoir, author.

People can maintain a white-hot level of concentration only so long. Eventually they must escape from the problem through friends, the outdoors, sleep, food and drink—sometimes excessively. These escapes are reported in the autobiographies of great creators. But even escape or retreat is occasionally productive.

Before the person returns to work—while on the beach, strolling along the street, playing some sport, or conversing with a friend—an answer, apparently unsought, pops into view. Whether this is because the brain continued to work on the problem unconsciously, or because the body simply needed time to regenerate, or because the rest period allowed other associations to form in the mind, no one really knows.

What is well known is the value of an incubation stage, but ONLY AFTER the concentration stage. Those words are emphasized because

some people who consider themselves creative spend most of their time in the incubation stage—on the beach, in front of the television, socializing—to no avail. Incubation without previous concentration is merely sloth.

One specific benefit of incubation has been identified by research in the psychological laboratories of Princeton University. Dr. Sam Glucksberg has been studying how people solve puzzles requiring "creative" solutions. In one situation, for example, a person is given a screwdriver, some wire, and a circuit board, and asked to construct a simple electrical circuit. Eventually they discover that they do not have enough wire, and they have to use the screwdriver as a conductor to close the last gap in the circuit. Many people never consider using the tool in this unusual way.

This inability to consider uncommon uses for common objects is called *functional fixedness*, and Dr. Glucksberg has demonstrated that this *fixedness* gradually disappears in a period of incubation. That is, people who are "resting" from using a screwdriver are more likely to think of using it in unusual ways than are people who continue to use the screwdriver to drive screws. Incubation loosens the bonds holding us in habitual patterns.

Incidentally, those who solve the circuit board puzzle fastest are those who have been encouraged to use the screwdriver for some other "non-screwdriver" task, such as slicing cheese.

PHASE FOUR—ILLUMINATION (AHA!)

> Most striking at first is this appearance of sudden illumination [in mathematical invention], a manifest sign of long, unconscious prior work. . . . These sudden inspirations never happen except after some days of voluntary effort which has appeared absolutely fruitless and whence nothing good seems to have come, where the way taken seems totally astray.
>
> H. Poincare, mathematician

The delicious part of creating—the dessert course—is what Arthur Koestler calls the AHA! stage when everything falls into place and the flashing light comes on. When AHAs come, they are intoxicating. Precisely because the bulb lights only after an intense period of concentration and frustration, its impact is enormous. After days, months, even years of tension over a problem, suddenly the answer shines like a beacon blazing in the night. The release is explosive; the intoxication of discovered new truth is as heady as love and wine. The euphoria is even greater in those cases where the idea springs directly from the unconscious unaided. While you were not even thinking about the problem, the solution—like an affectionate butterfly—floated gently up and landed on your shoulder.

The reaction is usually physical, the more so because creative people are outwardly expressive. They jump up, burst out of their door, and dash down the hall yelling, "I've got it," button-holing the nearest anybody to explain their solution to the closing problem, or the neat phrase they have just turned, or the exotic formula they have just honed.

PHASE FIVE—VERIFICATION/PRODUCTION

The need for a second period of conscious work, after the inspiration, is still easier to understand. It is necessary to put in shape the results of this inspiration, to deduce from them the immediate consequences, to arrange them, to word the demonstrations, but above all is verification necessary.

H. Poincare, mathematician

The AHA! stage, satisfying as it may be, is

only the end of the beginning. There is hard work yet to be done, and "hard work" is precisely the name for it. As the Red Queen said, any practiced person can think up six impossible things before breakfast. Testing them out, convincing everyone who needs to be convinced that the ideas are worth betting on, putting them into practice, locating the pluses and eliminating the dozens of small minuses—this final phase of the process requires persistence and more; people-oriented skills are required because most new ideas depend on other people for their eventual adoption. Many otherwise creative people flounder at this point; they don't have the persuasive and organizational abilities necessary to organize others into action.

The Characteristics of Creative People

Psychologists have long been fascinated by the nature of creativity and the kind of people who are the most creative. They generally agree that those creative in the arts and sciences have certain characteristics in common. Many people in other fields are also creative to a greater or lesser degree. While there has been less study of creativity in other fields (office workers, farmers, bus drivers, businessmen, teachers, factory employees) there is no reason not to assume that these characteristics apply to them as well. By developing these characteristics in yourself, you can increase your creativity.

The characteristics of creative people can be grouped generally into three categories:

Essential characteristics. Those that are crucial for the genesis of new ideas.

Enabling characteristics. Those necessary to keep creative ideas alive once they have been produced.

Subsidiary characteristics. Those that do not appear to have any place in either the creation or its sustenance but nevertheless often affect the behavior of the creator.

The **essential characteristics** are:

MENTAL AGILITY—CONVERGENT THINKING

Mental agility is the ability to play with ideas, concepts, symbols, words and numbers, and especially to be able to see unusual relationships between them. Convergent thinking is the ability to scan many relevant facts, then to zero in on those facts most likely to result in the correct solution to a particular problem. Creative people do this well, and this ability, like many physical abilities, holds up better when exercised. "Mental jogging" is as fruitful as physical jogging.

The following four puzzles with matches are problems requiring convergent thinking. They are mental exercises. A challenge is presented and a specific solution is required. You can play these puzzles on your kitchen table. Don't despair if you can't solve them immediately; they are difficult. Remember, you can't run a mile on the first trial either. Keep jogging!

The matches represent Roman numerals and are arranged in incorrect mathematical equations. Your task: "By moving one and only one match, change the incorrect equation into a correct one. . . ."

The first puzzle is:

$$IV = III + III$$

By moving one and only one match, make this into a correct equation.

The answer is below; try to solve it before you look.

The answer to puzzle #1, a simple one, is:

$$VI = III + III$$

The only difficulty is remembering your Roman numerals well enough to know that IV = 4 and VI = 6.

The second puzzle, slightly harder, is:

$$VII + V = I$$

There are two possible answers; they are found immediately below. Try to work it out before looking.

An answer to the second puzzle is:

$$VII - VI = I \qquad \text{or} \qquad VII - V = II$$

44

This puzzle is more complicated than the first one because you have to do more than just tinker with numbers; an algebraic sign must be changed. You have to veer away from "straight ahead" thinking to consider other possibilities out in left field, and that greatly reduces the number of people who successfully solve this puzzle because many people have given up "left field thinking."

The third puzzle, same rule, is:

$$\text{II} = \sqrt{\text{I}}$$

Don't look at the answer below until you've tried to solve it.

The solution to the third puzzle is:

$$\text{I} = \sqrt{\text{I}}$$

This solution is much more complicated because it requires the use of the square root sign ($\sqrt{}$). The flexibility to use matches for symbols other than numbers is still required, and to that is added the need for more mathematical sophistication—the ability to work with the square root sign.

One final puzzle, same rule: and the solution is immediately below the puzzle. By now you know you have to consider the unusual. The fourth puzzle is:

$$\frac{XXIII}{VII} = II$$

The answer to the fourth puzzle is:

$$\frac{XXII}{VII} = \overline{II}$$

This is an exceedingly complex answer; you must know that $\frac{22}{7} = 3.14 = \pi$ (*Pi*), and not everyone will know that. To reach this answer you have to be familiar with mathematical symbols, and you have to have the mental agility to find an unusual combination of those symbols—in short, your thinking has to be in shape, in good condition.

If you are out of shape, start slow, don't get discouraged, reward yourself for small successes, and stay with it.

MENTAL AGILITY—DIVERGENT THINKING

Divergent thinking is the ability to fan out in all directions from an idea. It is the opposite of convergent thinking. Instead of homing in one correct answer, divergent thinking helps you find several different answers.

For example, in response to the question:

"What would happen if everyone had an extra thumb, directly across from the existing one?"

divergent thinkers might rattle off answers such as:

"It would greatly expand the possibilities for intricate fingering of musical instruments."

"I could throw a curve ball easier."

"Carpenters would like it because if they smashed a thumb while nailing, they'd have a spare one right there."

"Sixgun revolvers would have a hammer on the bottom as well as the top."

"The nursery rhyme would be about twelve little Indians."

"We could swim better because of the added hand surface, and because if we had two extra thumbs, we'd probably have two extra big toes which means our feet would be better flippers."

All of these answers illustrate the rapid and resourceful output by people using divergent thinking.

CONCEPTUAL FLEXIBILITY

This is the flexibility to switch gears or approaches easily, spontaneously.

Some years ago in the course of research concerning the effect of conventional thinking of problem-solving ability, a clever test was given to a number of different groups. A pipe, sealed at the bottom, was placed upright on a table and a ping-pong ball was dropped into it. The problem was to get the ball back out of the pipe without turning the pipe over. (The pipe was too narrow to reach down inside.) Some of those asked for a solution were supplied with a pitcher of ice water and drinking glasses, while others were given a washbucket filled with water. The groups that had the bucket almost always thought of pouring the water into the pipe to bring the ball to the top, but those with the ice water usually drank up their solution while thinking about their seemingly impossible task.

The point is that it was easy for most people to connect the water in the bucket with the pipe, but it took really *flexible* thinkers to consider using the ice water as a tool.

ORIGINALITY

This is the ability to produce unusual ideas—not necessarily good ideas, but rare, even weird ideas. When asked, for example, "How many different uses can you think of for a 12 x 12 inch piece of aluminum foil?"

Most people give answers such as:

"Use it to reflect sunlight onto paper and twigs to start a fire."

or

"Wrap food in it for freezing."

I'M USING this ALUMINUM FOIL AS PART OF AN EXPERIMENTAL ATTEMPT to substitute SOLAR energy FOR excessive RELIANCE ON FOSSIL FUELS

CAN I have a little to wrap Leftovers?

Original thinkers come up with:

"Use it to measure the number of square feet in an underwater grotto, where wooden rulers would float to the surface."

"Grind it up for eyeshadow."

"Make a lapel handkerchief for a window

display where the mannequins are made up to look like people from Mars."

"Cut a smiling face in it and put it in the bottom of your briefcase so that when you take it through the airport x-ray security machine, the guard will get a smile."

"Use it to wrap around cigarettes to make them 'formal' cigarettes."

Deep inside most people there lurks a mischievous child. Sometimes this can result in bizarre examples of creativity. An example of such originality is a Texas millionaire by the name of Stanley Marsh. He first attracted my attention when I read an article about his "planted" Cadillacs. Intrigued by the tailfins of the 1950's Cadillacs, he bought several sedans and buried them headfirst with their fins sticking out along the driveway into his Texas home. To approach his house, you drive through a mini-grove of vertical Cadillacs.

Another story described his treatment of someone who parked in his reserved parking space. Instead of calling a tow truck, Marsh called a welder and had the miscreant's front bumper welded to a light pole.

By far the most startling story of Stanley Marsh's innovative energy has to do with the monkey scuba divers. The story is that Marsh has a private lake within his land, marked with "No Trespassing" signs. One day he noticed some trot lines, a Southern phrase for fishing lines left in overnight. Instead of calling the law to deal with the trespassing and illegal fishing,

Marsh went to a local medical school, secured the bodies of two monkeys that had been used in medical research, took them to a local scuba diving shop, had them outfitted with miniature scuba diving tanks, masks, and flippers, and returned with them to his lake. He pulled up the trot lines, fastened a monkey on each of them, and threw the lines back into the water.

Can you imagine the look on the fisherman's face the next day?

A PREFERENCE FOR COMPLEXITY OVER SIMPLICITY

Many groups of creative people have been thoroughly studied at the University of California's Berkeley campus; one clear finding was that creative individuals prefer complexity over simplicity. For example, when shown pictures such as the following

51

and asked to choose between them, they preferred the complicated, ambiguous sketches. Their equally competent but less innovative colleagues more often chose the simple, symmetrical drawings.

This preference of creative people for entangled intricacy extended into other portions of their lives, sometimes at the cost of considerable personal turmoil, but broadening their range of experience. As a result, they came into contact with more unusual ideas, weird associations, and "creativity," than did those who stayed with the safe and predictable.

Minds that wander through complex orchards are more likely to produce creative fruit. It takes rich associations to produce comments such as, "My foot's asleep—my toes feel like ginger ale," or "You know what that oil on that puddle reminds me of—a dead rainbow."

Frank Barron, the University of California psychologist who did this research, has said that "the preference for complexity allows the greatest possible richness of experience, even though discord and disorder result." His work indicates that the original person, in adulthood, often likes things messy, at least at first.

STIMULATING BACKGROUNDS

Creative thinkers usually have spent a long time with people who are good models of continual learning, constantly seeking stimulation.

They tend to grow up in families with many effective adults—parents, grandparents, aunts

Wow, I bet your Breath keeps your Nose from getting cold, and your teeth Must be good for opening cans.

and uncles, older brothers and sisters. The presence of such people in a child's life produces at least two useful outcomes: First, the child learns specific skills; second, the adults provide models of achievement for the child to follow. Each child varies, of course, but certain core features will be visible in most effective people—self-control, self-discipline, constant achievements, resilience in the face of failure, a sense of humor, curiosity. Children can be exposed to these in other settings too, but the home seems to be the most powerful learning environment.

MULTIPLE SKILLS

Creative people often have several skills. Woody Allen—actor, television and movie writer, author, director—plays the clarinet well enough to perform with the New Orleans Preservation Hall jazz band.

Frank Stanton—president of CBS television during its growth years—is a superb craftsman in wood.

Athelstan Spilhaus—scientist, administrator, oceanographer—designs celestial clocks and writes comic strips.

B. F. Skinner—perhaps the world's most famous psychologist and Harvard professor—is an excellent pianist.

Picasso—the famous artist—worked in many media, sketches, oil, and sculptures, including metal, wood, and marble.

Mary Tyler Moore—television's light comedy star—is an outstanding singer and dancer, and is financially astute enough to build the Mary Tyler Moore Enterprises.

R. B. Cattell—a noted personality theorist, psychological test author, and Professor Emeritus of Psychology from the University of Illinois—is a talented sailor and cement mason, and has constructed a scale replica of the English Channel in concrete in the backyard of his Illinois home.

Liv Ullman—one of the leading actresses in the world—has written a bestseller.

Dusty Rumsey—my son's 17-year-old friend and the most creative teenager I know—has won several statewide art contests, edited a creative high school yearbook, rejuvenated his van including upholstery and stereo installation, backpacked through the Linville Gorge, had the first public exhibition of his works—where he sold several thousand dollars worth of paintings—and was selected as his high school's most outstanding athlete for his prowess in soccer and basketball.

The benefit of multiple skills is obvious; people who have several skills don't get locked into a single path. They have several different paths available to them. More than that—their skills are enriched. A writer who is also a musician hears rhythms in the words that are not evident to others. An executive who is intimately familiar with the patterns of wood grains may see different possible arrangements of work

groups. A psychologist who also molds clay may have ideas about the malleability of human nature that are different from his colleagues who do not have sculpturing talents. An artist who climbs mountains may be familiar with more textures than an artist who doesn't climb.

To have only one skill forces you into a narrow approach to the world. People who are only good with hammers see every problem as a nail.

Enabling characteristics (those necessary to keep creative ideas alive once they have been produced) are:

CAPACITY FOR HARD WORK

Even the greatest musical geniuses have sometimes worked without inspiration. This guest does not always respond to the first invitation. We must *always* work, and a self-respecting artist must not fold his hands on the pretext that he is not in the mood. If we wait for the mood, without endeavoring to meet it halfway, we easily become indolent and apathetic.

Peter Ilich Tchaikovsky, composer

When creative people describe themselves, they always use some variation of "I simply work harder than anybody else." They toil long hours—literally living in their creative arena; whether it be art, science, marketing, or developing new products, their work consumes their lives. Blasé people rarely join the ranks of creators. A new idea—a new work of art, a new discovery in science, or an innovative corporate plan—requires enormous amounts of energy, time, and dedication. Consequently, wherever you find creative people, you also find hard workers.

Dede Allen, an outstanding film editor, was recently interviewed on the television show "Today." She was asked how she condensed hours of movie footage into a two- or three-minute segment; the example under discussion was a battle scene where three hours of action

WHAT ARe YOU WAITING FOR?

had been filmed to create one fast-moving minute in the eventual movie.

Her answer was: "I memorized all of the footage."

Interviewer: "The entire three hours?!"

Allen: "The entire three hours. I ran the film over and over and over, until I knew every nuance—then combined the best shots into the final one minute."

For Dede Allen, often honored as one of the world's most creative film editors, that creative act was mostly drudgery.

The inventor Thomas Edison said:

Invention is the hardest kind of work and requires intense application of every faculty. There is no guesswork about it. There is no unfailing principle of luck to it. The goal must be reached by a process of elimination. Every factor must be studied, examined, and then eliminated if it is not what you want, until you have narrowed the entire problem down to two or three points. Then it is possible that luck or accident may play a minor part, and some day the whole thing will dawn upon your mind and you see the goal you have been working for.

INDEPENDENT JUDGMENT

PLAYBOY: Do you care what other people think
about your work?

CAPOTE: I don't give a damn, really. I know
what I think about myself as a writer.
The fact is I'm very good.

Truman Capote, interview in *Playboy,*
Copyright © 1976 by Playboy

Creative people maintain a strong sense of individuality. They make their own decisions; they trust their own judgments.

To study independence of judgment, psychologists have devised a subtle test of how much a person is influenced by the opinions of others. Six people are seated in a room, supposedly for a visual acuity test. One of the group is the person under scrutiny. Unknown to this person, everyone else has been instructed to give fake answers. A slide with two lines—Line A and Line B—is flashed on the wall, with Line B being clearly longer. Each person is asked which line they think is longer, and everyone answering ahead of the selected person responds "Line A," which is obviously incorrect. This creates a dilemma for the selected person who sees that although Line B is clearly longer, everyone else has chosen Line A. In this situation, many people ignore what their own eyes tell them, cave in to group pressure, and go along with the majority opinion even though it directly conflicts with what they see.

When placed in such predicaments, people with creative achievements do not bow to group pressure. They report their own opinions and stick to them. They are not easily swayed, even by the combined judgments of others.

At their best, creative people provide a strong anchor in the midst of confusion; they are not sidetracked by minor distractions. They are unswervingly consistent, powered by their deep certainty that they are right.

At their worst, such people are rigid, locked into impossible plans that may destroy them and all around them. The different drummer they are marching to can march them right over the cliff into the sea like lemmings driven by an inexorable and fatal instinct.

This driving independence is not an essential ingredient in the creative process; rather it provides the persistence necessary to turn creative ideas into practical products. Creating new ideas can be relatively easy; turning them into useful products is quite another matter. The world is filled with divergent thinkers without this fierce need to be their own person, to fight the crowd, to pull their ideas through no matter what; without this persistence, their ideas go nowhere.

There is also the other extreme: firm-minded, strong-willed, independent people who are not interested in new ideas. Independence without creativity is usually insensitive and thoughtless, or at its best, mundane. Not only are such people uncreative, but they kill the creativity around them. Being independent is no guarantee for being innovative; one has to be sensitive to new ideas also.

I am neither stupid nor scared, and my sense of my own importance to the world is relatively small. On the other hand, my sense of my own importance to myself is tremendous. I am all I have, to work with, to play with, to suffer and to enjoy. It is not the eyes of others that I am wary of, but my own. I do not intend to let myself down more than I can possibly help, and I find that the fewer illusions that I have about me or the world around me, the better company I am for myself.

Noel Coward,
playwright

RESILIENCE

Partly because they keep their own counsel and are not overly concerned with the opinions of others and partly because they have a good opinion of themselves because of past successes, creative people are not easily discouraged by failure. They are resilient, willing, even eager, to try again. Sometimes they don't even see failure as failure, but simply another irritating, frustrating by-way on the road to success.

> With the good people, you can see the learning juices churning around every mistake. You learn from mistakes. When I look back, my life seems to be an endless chain of mistakes.
>
> Edward Johnson, a
> millionaire businessman

GOOD COMMUNICATORS

The most brilliant creator in the world without the ability to communicate would be ineffective. Among people who have achieved creative success, you find good communicators; indeed, in some fields—literature, drama, the media—creativity is synonymous with communicating. However, even in such fields as science and architecture, the most creative professionals are good communicators, and, importantly, they enjoy it. On tests of vocational interests, they usually report that they especially enjoy writing or speaking.

Again, these are *enabling* skills; the creator uses them to call the world's attention to a particular act of creativity.

INTERESTED MORE IN
CONCEPTS THAN IN DETAILS

Creative people do not get hung up early on the details of a project. They are more interested in a broad conceptual approach. For example, when attacking the problem of litter, they are less concerned with specific garbage items—cans, bottles, cigarette butts, paper—than with finding a general approach to the overall problem. Instead of focusing on individual details, they ask broad questions, such as, "How can we make litter into an attractive substance?" and their initial answers might be wildly improbable:

> "Put flower seeds in cigarettes so that every time a cigarette butt is thrown away, a flower is planted."

> "Design pay phones to accept old beer cans as well as dimes—then everyone would gather up the empty cans to use in making long distance calls."

The details of putting those ideas into practice do not bother them, at least at first. The general concept—making litter into an attractive substance—is the important point; that approach might lead to more creative solutions.

INTELLECTUALLY CURIOUS

Creative people have unending curiosity about their part of the world, about their environment. They are constantly asking, "What's

that?" "What if . . . ?" "Why?" They wonder what makes things work, what makes organizations successful, what creates the Northern Lights, why mirrors reverse images from left to right but not top to bottom, why when you want something up, you don't "higher" it—if you want it down, you lower it. They are always questioning, seeking information, pondering paradoxes.

We all asked those questions as children but we tend to lose this curiosity as we grow up. In this sense, life can be divided into three stages:

Ages 1-7 = WHY?
7-17 = WHY NOT?
17-70 = BECAUSE

I'D LiKE to TALK to the ANswer DepartMent... I'd Like to know Why Birds sing; WHy FooLs FALL IN LoVE; ANd WHAt the New model cars will Look Like.

A specific example of childish curiosity at work happened to a friend of mine; he tells this story about his 10-year-old:

Some friends came home with us one night for a visit. I filled some glasses with ice from the refrigerator and mixed us all a drink. As we sat there, talking and sipping, I thought that mine tasted strange, a bit salty. I ignored it, but the salt taste got stronger. Then one of my friends said, "What did you mix my drink with, sea water? It tastes funny."

I said, "So does mine; I don't know what happened—let me mix you another." So I mixed another round, but in a few minutes we had the same problem—the drinks still tasted salty.

I'm not sure we would have ever figured out the trouble if Sandy, our 10-year-old, hadn't come in just then, opened the refrigerator door, and asked, "Who took my ice cubes?" So the story came out. "My teacher said that salt water wouldn't freeze, so I was trying it out. I put different amounts of salt in several ice cube trays to see what would happen—what did you do with all the trays?"

These parents were proud of their child's curiosity and took the episode in stride. The point: If you are going to live around creative people, you must occasionally expect a few salty ice cubes.

PLAYFUL, SPONTANEOUS

Might we not say that every child at play behaves like a creative writer, in that he creates a world of his own or, rather, rearranges the things of his world in a new way which pleases him? It would be wrong to think he does not take that world seriously; on the contrary, he takes his play very seriously and he expends large amounts of emotion on it.

Sigmund Freud

Many creative people have a strong sense of humor and a rich fantasy life. They seek out whimsy and are relatively uninterested in policing their own thoughts, emotions, and impulses.

They are, in a word, playful, and their playfulness brings them into contact with a wider range of life than people who lead staid, "adult" lives—and this wider range leads them into more creative enterprises. Chapter Six has a longer discussion of the value of play in creativity.

The playfulness of creative people does not always fit into socially acceptable patterns. An example is reported in David Niven's marvelous book, *Bring on the Empty Horses,* a collection of anecdotes and nostalgia from his days in Hollywood:

> [Humphrey Bogart] had a predilection for that particular Elizabethan [four-letter] word and enjoyed the shock waves it could produce when used to the greatest effect. We once spent an afternoon in 21 in New York, flanked by [some of Hollywood's greatest writers], drinking stingers and poring over various telephone directories. We worked out that by forging the signature of the Con Edison Company and sending 438 telegrams to selected officeholders in Radio City requesting them, for testing purposes, to leave their lights blazing at the end of the day, we could emblazen the word in letters sixteen floors high.

The urge of creative people to spell out four-letter words in squirrelly ways appeared in a recent novel. In one episode, a particularly talented character proposes selling opera tickets to bald-headed men in a pattern so arranged that when they take their seats on the main floor, those in the balconies would be treated to the startling sight of gleaming bald domes spelling out a four-letter word several rows high. The honor of dotting the "i" in this barnyard word was to be reserved for a man who was a particular object of scorn.

When creative people congregate, humor of dubious propriety will occasionally erupt, to the discomfort of those in charge. If you are part of, or responsible for, a group of people charged with the development of new ideas, and your group is free from such improprieties, you had better worry—your group is probably too restrained for white-hot creativity.

THEY AVOID EARLY SELF-CRITICISM OF THEIR IDEAS

When truly creative people come up with a new idea, they do not reject it immediately because of its flaws. They play with it, looking for strengths and sliding over weaknesses. They don't need to be immediately right, especially where their own thoughts are concerned. In contrast, people who seldom pull off anything novel approach new ideas from the opposite viewpoint: "What's wrong with this idea? Where can we get into trouble? How can things go wrong?" Remember the wheelbarrow? Most of us think that way unless we guard against it.

A SENSE OF DESTINY

I did not make my songs, my songs
made me.

Goethe

. . . Without this intense cosmological
commitment, no amount of mental ability
. . . will produce a genuinely creative act.
Without wishing to be overly dramatic in this
matter, I believe it is literally true that creative individual[s] are willing to stake [their]
lives on the meaning of [their] work.

Frank Barron, psychologist

Creative people often exhibit what Professor Donald MacKinnon of the University of California, Berkeley—a creativity expert—calls a "sense of destiny." They see themselves as the right person with the right idea in the right place at the right moment in history. Creating is their fate. Their creations are not to be challenged because "they were meant to be." They may even explain their power to create as a mystical force acting through them—God, some cosmic entity, "The Muse," or "an inner devil."

This intuition of being more in tune with some ethereal spirit than the average person is a characteristic that the great creator shares with the great leader—and one that is useful to both. The "sense of destiny" creates a momentum that fuels persistence, overcomes failures, and persuades ordinary mortals to do the leader's or creator's will.

In humane and decent people this mystic motivation can be an enormous force for progress: new ideas, new freedoms, new beauties, and new philosophies that spring forth to create entire new cultures. But in talented psychopaths this "sense of destiny" can plunge organizations, cultures, nations, even the world, into total chaos.

Subsidiary characteristics (those that have nothing to do with the creation or its sustenance but do affect the creators' behavior). Many extremely creative people have qualities which make them unpredictable, hard to live with, and hard to manage, qualities that are not necessary for creativity, but which seem to be by-products.

UNCONCERN OVER WHAT OTHERS THINK

Creative people think for themselves. They are not concerned with the opinions of others and consequently may be insensitive to the feelings of those around them. Because they do not adopt the little niceties of social convention, they may appear weird, unsociable, abrasive.

> Rachmaninoff strode into the Edison recording studios and sat down at the piano. He was there to make a trial record. The inventor shuffled in close behind him. "Go ahead," said Edison. The massive hands moved over the keyboard in the grand Romantic style typical of Rachmaninoff.
>
> Edison interrupted: "Who told you you're a piano player? You're a pounder—that's what you are, a pounder!" Without a word, Rachmaninoff got up from the bench, put on his hat, and walked out.
>
> Bridget Paolucci,
> "Edison as Record Producer"

PSYCHOLOGICAL TURBULENCE

Because they seek complexity, have strong egos, do not curb their impulses, and care little for the opinions of others, creative people are often in the midst of psychological turbulence. Their marriages break up, they become alcoholic, they commit suicide, they lose their jobs.

This does not mean that all divorcees, alcoholics, unemployed, and suicidal people are creative. But these situations are relatively common among people who are.

Living by unusual rules and viewing the world through a different set of filters can lead to an internal state, described by my colleague Jenny Godwin, who teaches creative problem solving, as a "steady state of storms."

These characteristics taken alone do not lead to innovative outputs. This point needs to be emphasized because I know at least one professional who, after studying the research findings of psychologists, deliberately set out to be weird, abrasive, insensitive to others, justifying this behavior as part of the "creative career."

Unfortunately, his level of creativity comes nowhere close to excusing these actions.

The useful traits of creative people—the ability to think fluently, the wide range of skills and experiences, the ability to see new ideas in old procedures—have nothing to do with this last group of irascible characteristics. The latter emerge only because of the powerful personality of creative people, and the emotional strain of creativity. The difficult flood of behavior is only a troublesome by-product of the creative spring.

Professor Paul Torrance from the University of Georgia, one of the world's leading experts on creative children, spoke directly to this point in one of his studies. (I have paraphrased him slightly here.)

We formed groups of five children, placing in each group one of the most creative children in the class, then gave them a puzzle requiring creative thinking and group competition. The results suggest that highly creative individuals may be responsible for most of their own woes. . . .

At the second-grade level, the most highly creative individuals were generally unpleasant, showed little consideration for the group, little goal orientation, little identification with the group, and paid little or no heed to the leadership attempts of their less creative peers. . . . These tendencies became more pronounced in the sixth-grade groups.

The problem is to help highly creative students retain those characteristics essential for creative talent, and at the same time help them acquire diplomatic skills for getting along with their classmates.

What Kind of Families Produce Creative Children

What are the characteristics of families that produce creative children? What follows is based on averages calculated over many people; obviously, no one family exactly fits this composite. Indeed, many families contradict it in many ways—still, the trends are important. Much of what follows is based on the research of Professor Donald MacKinnon and his colleagues at the University of California, Berkeley, in their extensive studies of creative people—writers, mathematicians, architects, artists, and scientists.

RESPECT FOR THE CHILD AS A PERSON

Parents of creative children value them as important individuals. Early in life they are treated as an equal member of the family. Their opinions are listened to and acted upon. They are allowed to make their own decisions about such matters as what to wear, when to go to bed, and what school subjects to take. Gradually they become important contributors in the family decision-making.

This approach has two important outcomes: First, the child develops a healthy sense of self-esteem. While virtually all parents value their children highly, many are so uncommunicative that the child doesn't realize the depth of the parental love and affection. Children are not sure that you love them unless you tell them so directly, and then treat them accordingly. Parents of creative children do that.

MY Daughter WeNt CAMPING. SHE PIHCHED A TENT, CAUGHT A FiSH, ANd STARTED A FIRE WITH 2 STONES

Second, through the experience of sharing responsibility in a closely monitored environment, the child learns to make good decisions. In contrast, in families who keep their children on short reins, seventeen- or eighteen-year-olds away from home for the first time suddenly confront a range of choices: how to spend their time, how to use their money, what kind of relationships to enter and how to behave in them. The results can be catastrophic; the parents have been so restrictive that the child has been denied the opportunity to learn to think independently.

Parents of creative children give them early opportunities to experiment, to make mistakes and learn from them when the stakes are not

I DON'T LET MY DAUGHTER CROSS THE STREET ALONE

large. When the important choices come later, the child has a base of self-confidence to deal from, and some actual "hands-on" experience in living with the results of their own decisions. This treatment of the children by parents probably leads to the extraordinary sense of autonomy exhibited later by creative adults.

In her marvelous autobiography *Portrait of Myself*, Margaret Bourke-White says, "Learning to do things fearlessly was considered important by both my parents. Mother had begun

when I was quite tiny to help me over my childish terrors, devising simple little games to teach me not to be afraid of the dark, encouraging me to enjoy being alone instead of dreading it, as so many children and some adults do." From that beginning, she went on to become a world-renowned photographer.

AN EXPECTATION OF REASONABLE
AND RESPONSIBLE BEHAVIOR

This freedom to make decisions is accompanied by a strong expectation that the child will make reasonable, responsible ones. The parents know what is going on and provide guidance and limits to the child's behavior—it is not an uncaring, permissive arrangement, but rather one which gives the child latitude with accountability.

GOOD ADULT MODELS

Children who later become creative adults tend to grow up in families where there is a plentiful supply of good adult models of effectiveness—sometimes the mother, sometimes the father, sometimes other adults in an extended family such as aunts, uncles, or grandparents. Somewhere in the child's life is a highly achieving adult for them to observe. Children without such a model in their own family frequently find one elsewhere in the form of a mentor—a teacher, a coach, a first employer— but parents can serve this role best because they are quite literally closer to home.

CONSIDERABLE FAMILY MOBILITY

The parents of creative people move more often than their colleagues, both from place to place within a city, and from city to city. This mobility probably reflects both the parents' level of achievement—they are moving to take advantage of better opportunities—and some innate, restless adventuresomeness on their part—they are not content to remain forever in any one situation.

The impact is two-fold: first, in a generally positive way, the moves bring increased stimulation and experience. Children who are familiar with, say, both the Midwest and the East Coast have a greater store of knowledge to draw from than do those who have spent their entire lives in one location. Second, in perhaps a negative way, the children are denied the luxury of long-term unbroken friendships. They learn early that friendships are not permanent. This realization, consciously or unconsciously, again probably contributes to the sense of autonomy usually found in creative adults.

This is not to suggest that hauling kids around the country, moving them out of their neighborhoods, tearing them away from their friends will alone make them more creative. But if other essential and enabling personal and environmental factors are present, family mobility can be another ingredient in producing a creative adult.

CONCERN FOR THE DEVELOPMENT OF TALENT

The parents of future creative people value achievement. They encourage the development of talents at early ages, especially in the artistic and intellectual areas. While they seldom "hotbox" their children—hovering over them constantly to make certain that they are reading, studying, or practicing—they do create the kind of atmosphere that favors continual learning and striving. In reading the descriptions of family environments of the people in the California studies, you can almost feel the vibrations in the air that led the children to seek out their own areas to be active and excel in. Musical instruments, scientific experiments, books, machines, art supplies, and plenty of adults using them were common in their homes.

CLEAR ETHICAL STANDARDS

There was often within these families clear standards of right and wrong, and family discipline was consistent and predictable. But coupled with this was the expectation that the children would work through their beliefs for themselves and not follow the parents blindly.

The families of future creative adults tended to have strong feelings about their standards. Often these standards conflicted with the popular opinions about politics, religion and morals. But the emphasis, nevertheless, was on the children developing their own rules and codes of behavior.

Among the values most often stressed in these families were:

Integrity—being honest and forthright.

Appreciation of quality—taking joy in craftsmanship, and the development of talents; pride in themselves and their efforts.

Intellectual curiosity—an interest in ideas, solving problems, literature, music, the arts, the sciences, and reading for pleasure.

Ambition—a concern for making something out of life, for achievement, for getting good grades, for winning recognition, for taking care of oneself.

LACK OF ANXIOUS CONCERN FOR THE CHILD

Perhaps the last point that should be made, especially for the benefit of parents who are reading this and wondering what they should be doing with, or for, their children is that the parents of creative children were generally relatively relaxed about their children. They did not sit up nights wringing their hands, wondering how things were going to turn out. Nor did they let their own lives revolve around those of their children. Generally, they followed their own effective careers, provided physical and intellectual stimulation for their families, and emphasized certain philosophies in life. Then—as far as raising the children was concerned—they let the chips from the block fall where they may.

AIDS IN RAISING CREATIVE CHILDREN

The best advice is probably Benjamin Franklin's comment: "What you do speaks so loudly, I cannot hear what you are saying." Exhorting your children to be better, more creative, more innovative, is of little avail unless you live that way yourself.

Lead an active life. Surround your children with stimulation in the form of:

- **Ideas.** Let them know what you think about the important topics in life—sex, money, marriage, your job, religion; make certain they understand that these are only your ideas, not necessarily TRUTH. Other people have other viewpoints.

- **Stimulating gifts.** Money helps, but imagination and energy are more important. Give them books and help them write their own. Buy them boats or help them build their own. Get them scientific gadgets, sewing machines, tickets to operas, plays, concerts, and lectures (there are lots of free ones), hand tools, exotic

plants and musical instruments, especially homemade ones. Help them learn how to use these things.

- **Innovative adults.** Introduce them to your colleagues and other interesting people. Your kids enjoy stimulating lunches too, as long as they are treated as real people and not just appendages.

- **Travel.** Let them move around; anywhere, even the next neighborhood, is stimulating if you have never been there before. An Arabic proverb says:

ان كنت تحب اولادك دعهم
يمارسون سفريّاتهم

"If you love your children, send them on their travels."

- **Develop their fantasy.** Encourage their imagination. Encourage them to think: "What if . . . ?"; and to make up their own stories and appreciate the creations of others.

Then, relax! What you do deliberately probably doesn't make that much difference anyway.

CHAPTER 6

Seven Blocks to Creativity in Organizations

Most of us live, work, and play in organizations of one kind or another: schools, companies, teams, churches, agencies, lodges, corporations. Such groups can help or hinder our creativity in various ways. Following are seven common organizational barriers. If you understand them, you can more easily get around them—or, if you are in charge, eliminate them.

BLOCK ONE—FEAR OF FAILURE

Fear of failure affects organizations in three damaging ways: first, in determining who is rewarded for what; second, in creating pressure for immediate success; and third, in demanding predictable outcomes.

The reward structure. In most organizations, the penalties for failure are much greater than the rewards for success. In fact, the penalties for failure are usually greater than the penalties for doing nothing at all. Consequently, workers either choose safe alternatives or do nothing . . . they still get paid . . . so why take a chance! As one manager said, "When the winds of change blow through, I just turn up my collar, put my back to the wind, and hunker down until that particular storm blows over. The people who last around here are the ones who don't screw up, not those who create fresh breezes."

Pressure for immediate results. While success almost always requires long-range efforts by many people, failure is immediately possible and usually focused on one person. In fear-of-failure organizations, people focus on pro-

grams that are short and will produce something, however ordinary. They may not succeed very well but they don't fail.

The certainty of predictability. Where failure is punished, people act only when the outcomes are highly predictable. They don't want to be surprised. In such settings, routine, predictable programs are preferred over innovative, unpredictable ones because the routine programs produce fewer failures. Anyone arguing for new ways with absolute candor— "I think it will work, but I can't be sure"— appears not only indecisive but irrational. Innovators who work in failure-fearing environments know the sweaty-palm feeling of arguing forcefully outside—"I *know* this will work; it's got everything going for it"—while inside quivering—"There are at least 16 iffy things here that could get my neck stretched."

If you can't confidently predict success, many organizations will ask you to seek employment elsewhere. Because most management control systems focus on predictable outcomes—Management by Objectives, Planned Results —most innovative people don't feel comfortable working within them so they do move on. The demand for *predictable* outcomes deprives many companies of *unusual* outcomes. Innovation is seldom predictable.

Of course, fear of failure is not all bad; mistakes are, after all, not nice things to have around. In some settings—on airplanes, in submarines, in coal mines—they are catastrophic. The trick is to give failure its due, but no more. Failures and successes are intimate relatives; if you want to dine with the latter, you must occasionally sit down with the former, especially as you sometimes can't tell them apart until about the third course.

BLOCK TWO—
A PREOCCUPATION WITH ORDER AND TRADITION

Order is important, even vital, but if everything happens according to plan, there is no innovation. Tradition and order usually go hand-in-hand because the most orderly way of doing something is to do it the way it was done before. This places excessive reverence on the past and creates conformity when it is not necessary, or even effective. While tradition produces stability, it may also produce stagnancy.

An obsession with order also reflects a fear of messiness in relationships between people; non-traditional arrangements are scary. Children shouldn't be found in working organizations; they are unpredictable. Husbands and wives shouldn't work together; their relationship at home might complicate their work on the job. Men shouldn't report to women managers; they might be threatened by them. Older people should not report to younger people; their feelings might be hurt. The insistence on order and tradition goes on even though past practices may be constrictive, ineffective, discriminatory, and, perhaps, illegal.

The need for order also requires the elimination of strong emotions because they can be messy. Love, anger, euphoria, and depression have no place in organizations requiring order. Emotional stability is valued above all. Confusion, conflict, and ambiguity are avoided. If they do appear, they are kept closeted. These constrictions produce bland work settings, and bland work settings do not produce creative products.

Order is not all bad; sometimes it is desirable. One prefers dental work done in an office that is orderly. People want their taxes done by an orderly accountant. If people need brain surgery, they want it done in an operating room free of confusion. But in these three settings, precision is the goal, not innovation. Where innovation is common, messiness is usually a by-product.

BLOCK THREE—RESOURCE MYOPIA

This is the failure to see one's own strengths and the strengths of people around you. It is a lack of appreciation for resources, both people and things, in one's environment, and a lack of trust in human capacities and work styles that are different from your own.

Resource myopia is common among pragmatic, no-nonsense realists who "see things as they are." Innovation thrives on seeing things as they might be.

Organizations typically use only a fraction of the total talent available to them, and individuals typically use only a fraction of their talents on their jobs. Usually this is because people are slotted into specific jobs with traditional tasks. Their untraditional talents are never used. For example, a secretary who is skilled in conducting meetings is not allowed to use that talent because secretaries do not run meetings.

Formal chain-of-command organizations are particularly susceptible to resource myopia because of the intense pressure for people to play a role appropriate to their level. Unusual talents among junior-level workers are wasted.

BLOCK FOUR—
OVERCERTAINTY: THE SPECIALIST'S DISEASE

People who "really know" a subject—or think they do—are less open to new approaches. Experts are expert because they have been successful in the past with a certain approach to a problem. But because they have been well rewarded for their methods, they become reluctant to relinquish them. They persist in behavior that is no longer effective. What has been successful in the past becomes dogmatic and inflexible in the present.

History records a long list of innovations that came from outside the "expert" organization. The automobile was not invented by the transportation experts of that era, the railroaders. The airplane was not invented by automobile experts. Polaroid film was not invented by Kodak; handheld calculators were not invented by IBM; digital watches were not invented by watchmakers. The list is endless; and the moral vivid.

BLOCK FIVE—
RELUCTANCE TO EXERT INFLUENCE

Many people with good ideas do not wish to appear pushy and are hesitant to stand up for their own beliefs. Consequently, the most inno-

MR Potter Feels computers Are A Fad.

vative people in an organization are seldom the most forceful. They may in fact be withdrawn and particularly adverse to accumulating and exercising interpersonal power. Organizations are only as innovative as their most dominant people; ideas from others are lost in the "I'm not going to rock the boat" swamp.

BLOCK SIX—
A RELUCTANCE TO PLAY

The opposite of play is not what is serious
but what is real.

Sigmund Freud

In formal organizations, people are usually
overly serious. Because they do not wish to
appear foolish, they seldom try "what if" or
"let's pretend." Stuffy organizations do not culti-
vate people's fantasies and consequently are
deprived of the unusual thoughts that skitter
through people's imaginations—a substantial

loss because many established programs of today were once skittering fantasies.

Playfulness has its place, as is well documented in the animal kingdom. Play is an important learning method—in young animals, it is central in learning many skills that will eventually be critical for adult survival. Tiger cubs learn to stalk each other at play where errors don't matter; later, this skill helps them stay alive.

Three factors characterize play in animals; the same factors are probably important in creative organizations. First, animals at play are exuberant, energetic, active, always in motion, not inert, passive, or apathetic. The same patterns can be seen in creative people; most of them consider their work as "play," and, while they are doing it, they are exuberant, active, cheerful, alive. An organization that cannot tolerate playfulness will encourage apathy, inertness, a feeling of dullness.

Second, animals at play engage in actions similar to adult behavior, but with random sequencing. They are practicing the bits and pieces of adult life, but in no particular order. The cub may stalk another cub briefly, then engage in rough-and-tumble wrestling, then be distracted by a butterfly, then go back to stalking. The whole act has to eventually be pulled together correctly, but play allows for practice of isolated parts.

Third, young animals are able to play because someone else, usually the parents, serves the survival functions—gathering food, watching for danger, taking care of shelter. The analogy probably holds true in human organizations: Those at play, creating, need to be supported by other portions of the organization in carrying out the survival functions such as production, marketing, accounting, and personnel. The establishment of separate research laboratories is a direct example of the way to separate creative people from the survival functions.

Organizations that prohibit play are probably prohibiting creativity. If they don't need creativity, this is no problem but, if they do, the absence of play may eventually be lethal.

BLOCK SEVEN—
EXCESSIVE REWARD FOR SUCCESS

Strangely, when people are asked to solve problems requiring a creative solution, they are more successful when the stakes are low than when the stakes are high. In the example described earlier, students were asked to construct a simple electrical circuit, but were not given enough wire; they had to use their screwdriver for a purpose other than for what it was intended—the final link between terminals.

Students who were given the task simply as an interesting challenge succeeded more often than students who were told that they would be paid twenty-five dollars if they succeeded. The anxiety created by the opportunity to make a considerable sum interfered with their creative process.

The same phenomenon works in organizations where the payoffs are high. In television, the creative breakthroughs tend not to come in network programming, which must follow tried-and-true formulas, but rather in educational television or other settings where the stakes are not so high. Similarly, in big-time collegiate or professional athletics, successful teams seldom show the most razzle-dazzle. Usually they have a basic, thoroughly tested style and rarely deviate from it.

If you want creativity in your organization, you should do what you can to avoid these blocks.

Characteristics of Creative Managers

For organizations to be creative, the people who run them have to value innovation, and have to know how to deal with innovations when they come along. Following are the characteristics of managers who seem best able to do this.

WILLING TO ABSORB RISKS TAKEN BY SUBORDINATES

Managers who encourage creativity allow their people unusual freedom, expect that some errors will be made, and are able to absorb the inevitable failures. In contrast, managers who are afraid of mistakes will not defend failures to higher management. Instead, they restrict the freedom of their subordinates to experiment, hoping to keep all mistakes out of their lives. They will not allow risks to be taken, untested procedures to be tried, or "weird" activities to go on in their laboratories. As a consequence, the development of creative products is often restricted.

COMFORTABLE WITH HALF-DEVELOPED IDEAS

Managers of productive research laboratories can live with half-developed ideas. They do not insist that every *t* be crossed and every *i* be dotted before supporting an idea. They are willing to listen to, and support, "half-baked" proposals and encourage subordinates to press on. Of course, these managers have to have good instincts and good judgment. They can't allow every wild-eyed proposal to be carried out. They must have the ability to pick out those incomplete ideas that are worth pursuing. In contrast, some managers require that all questions be answered before allowing any new procedures to be considered. "Where's your cost estimates? How can we be sure it will·work? Have you thought of . . . (the 16 zillion things that can go wrong)?" These are reasonable questions but, when asked too early, they kill innovation.

WILLING TO "STRETCH" COMPANY POLICY

There are times in every organization when the company rulebook needs to be ignored. Creative managers have a feel for these times. They don't normally disregard rules and policies, but they do know when the rules need to be stretched for the greater good. Other managers, in contrast, are rulebook managers and will not permit any deviation, no matter what the possible payoff. If you always play by the book, you will win some important games, but your wins will be predictable, achievable by anyone else following the same book.

BOX SCORE

	1	2	3	4	5	6	7	8	9	Total
REALISTS	2	1	3	0	4	2	5	1	2	0
IDEALISTS	0	0	0	0	0	0	0	0	0	1

You can win the innings but still lose the game!

ABLE TO MAKE QUICK DECISIONS

When a new idea is presented to productive managers, they have the ability and willingness to make a decision on-the-spot without waiting for further studies, or for another committee, or for a new task force. They are ready to begin tomorrow, even this afternoon, if the idea has merit. They have good track records in recognizing which half-developed idea is worth betting on, and they are courageous enough to immediately commit resources to carrying it out.

GOOD LISTENERS

Productive managers listen to their personnel and build on their suggestions. They do not try

102

to ram new policies or procedures down the throats of people without listening to the other side first. In particular, they seem to have the ability to draw out the best in their subordinates and then add to it.

DON'T DWELL ON MISTAKES

Productive managers are more future-oriented than past-oriented. They do not wail over past mistakes—their own or others. Nor do they hold the mistakes of others against them indefinitely. They are willing to begin with the world as it is today and work for a better future. They learn from experience, but they do not wallow in it.

ENJOY THEIR JOB

Productive managers like what they are doing. They do not feel trapped in an administrative role. Rather, they enjoy the resources and power at their fingertips to push projects forward. In general, they are enthusiastic, invigorating individuals. They add to instead of subtract from the energy in their environments.

THE WORK SETTING—BEST FOR YOU

If you are a truly creative person and are looking for a setting that will encourage you, or if you are in charge of creative people trying to increase their creativity, you may simply need an environment free from bureaucracy, one tolerant of diverse behavior. When a wealthy patron once asked Pablo Picasso what he could do to help him, Picasso looked at him and said succinctly, "Stand out of my light."

In contrast, if you see yourself as productive but relatively unimaginative, and if you want more creativity in your life, you probably need to seek out a different sort of environment—one that places a premium on risk taking and innovation. You don't want a passive environment; you want an active one that will stretch you.

You may find new stimulation simply by changing environments: If you are working in the city, spend more time in the country; if you live in the country, spend some time in the heart of a large city. If you are working or studying in a small organization, find some way to wander around in a giant corporation. If you are familiar with huge companies, get acquainted with a small operation such as a one-person business or a travelling entrepreneur. With a little thought and effort, anyone should be able to find some new environments to experiment with. Such knowledge will be useful to you when you settle in one place, either as a worker or a manager.

The Creative Organization

To be more creative in organizations, to bring about change, is not always easy. The better we understand the relationship between creativity and leadership, the more successful we are likely to be.

Leadership can be represented by a bold arrow, signifying a forward thrust.

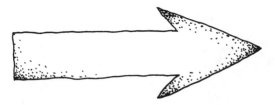

Creativity can be represented by a change in direction:

These symbols can be combined in various ways to represent different leadership styles.

Following are three diagrams representing three different combinations of leadership and creativity.

STRAIGHT ARROW—ORGANIZATION 1

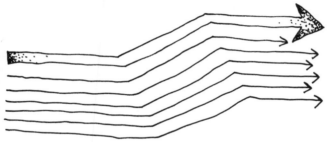

In Organization 1 the leadership is strong, and the people are conscientious and loyal, following orders from the top. When instructed to change directions, they do so quickly, firmly, and in concert. The result is a strong, united front, capable of moving great distances quickly. The purest illustration is a well-disciplined military unit under strong leadership. Another example is a highly trained athletic team. Where the challenges and opportunities for an organization require it to move quickly and forcefully in one direction, this is an effective arrangement.

107

A president of a large, successful company recently described this leadership style:

> Whoever is in charge has to have a clear idea of where the organization is going, and has to transmit that clearly to the workers. Leaders have to be so firmly convinced that their ideas are right—and I think mine are—that there is no doubt in anyone else's mind either. I'm quite willing to present my views—indeed, I insist on it—to my managers as a catechism to be memorized.
>
> You can't please everyone, so you had better say firmly, "This is a northbound train—if you wish to go south, you had better get off at the next station."

CROOKED ARROW—ORGANIZATION 2

In contrast, Organization 2 is filled with creative people shooting off in all directions, never powerfully, never organized, but in a continually exploring manner. They do not present any single, forceful front, yet they can be strong in their diversity; no matter which direction you look, someone is out in front. This arrangement is typical of most universities, where the arrows represent individual faculty members, and good research labs where the arrows represent individual scientists. Neither universities nor research labs are good at putting ideas into practice—for that, some strong arrows are needed—but they are outstanding in having a huge pool of ideas on virtually any topic of current or future interest. They are especially good at finding problems and opportunities that traditional "Type-1" organizations, filled with straight arrows, never see because of their narrower focus.

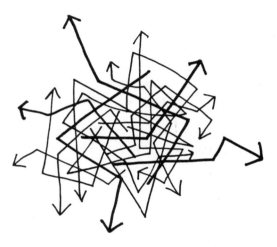

Organizations 1 and 2 are two different ways of life, and they attract people with different characteristics. The first attracts effective, efficient people who like a clear sense of where they are going, who feel pride in meeting practical goals, and who are uncomfortable in ambiguous, ill-defined settings. They are good team players and when there are no teams around, they get nervous.

In contrast, Organization 2 attracts creative people who dislike order and structure. They not only tolerate ambiguity but seek it out. They are skeptical of teamwork, cynical about leadership, and hostile toward authority. Because they are independent, they follow their own drummers, marching alone, at their own pace, into unexplored territory—occasionally, as with some tenured professors, never to be heard from again.

Members of Organization 1 (the straight arrows) who meet workers from Organization 2 (the crooked arrows) find them unrealistic, impractical, woolly-headed types who couldn't meet a payroll if Dear Abby herself handled the introductions.

Conversely, members of Organization 2 who meet workers from Organization 1 think they are rigid, unimaginative, goal-driven people, willing to sell all the fresh water and clean air in the world, along with their grandmothers, for a better looking balance sheet.

The two types do not mingle well.

COMBINATION—ORGANIZATION 3

The most dramatic progress occurs when the strengths of both approaches can be combined, as in Organization 3, where there is a creative person with the leadership skills to attract and guide others. Powerful, straight-ahead thrusts coupled with the broad coverage provided by a swarm of creative people—who are particularly useful in helping the powerful leader decide when to change directions—is the most effective structure for a creative organization.

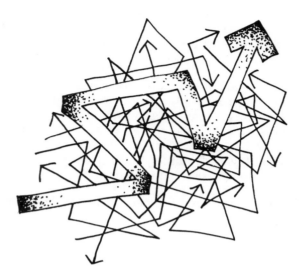

Without a strong central force, the swarm of creative people may wander around aimlessly, which is not all bad. Aimless wandering, done by people who are alert to new opportunities, can create new innovations—but before the new innovation can become a significant event, a big, bold arrow has to come along and pull, push, prod, and cajole it into practical reality.

Examples of such bold, creative arrows are Thomas Edison, Edward Land (father of the Polaroid camera), and Walt Disney. They have all been creative geniuses, strong leaders, and empire builders. What they accomplished was possible not only because they were creative, but also because they had the leadership skills to enlist the loyalty of both Types 1 and 2 into their projects.

Woody Allen, best known for his comic talents, is another prime example; about the leadership process, he says:

> The question is, do you want to take the time to get people around you who are not only very talented, but whom you can work well with ... I'm surrounded by lots of expertise in my films. I can tell those guys what I want, and then go back the next day and do it over ... if I change my mind.

One of the creative people who works with him says:

> It's the best fun working with Woody. He's instructive, hilarious, interesting. He's very gentlemanly, and there are never any arguments. Generally, one person is clearly right. Woody has the determination to sit and get the line right; he has faith in his own instincts.

Both quotes are from the excellent book about Woody Allen, *On Being Funny* by Eric Lax.

FROM LIGHT WEIGHT TO BIG BOLD ARROW

During the years ahead in your career—if you are creative—you are likely to play first the role of the lightweight arrow, out exploring new terrain and later on—if you accept more responsibility—the role of the bold, heavyweight arrow, making decisions and setting policy. When you join any organization where you are not the dominant force—whether it be your eighth-grade class, college fraternity, first em-

112

ployer, or as a newly elected member of Congress—you are automatically in the role of the lightweight arrow, with some concern for what is happening and some time to look around but without much clout. Later when you move into a more responsible position, whether as president of the Student Council or the president of a major corporation, you take on the powerful role of the Big Bold Arrow. Actually, if you are both creative and leadership oriented, you will sometimes play both roles simultaneously, either in different organizations, or at different times in the same organization. For maximum effectiveness, you should be able to play both roles, and if you do them well, the results will be exhilarating for you.

Nothing is more satisfying than to improve the world in ways that you approve of.

CHAPTER

9

Risk Taking: Physical and Financial, Intellectual and Sexual

Even if the breath of hope which blows on us from that new continent were fainter than it is and harder to perceive, yet the trial (if we would not bear a spirit altogether abject) must by all means be made. For there is no comparison between that which we may lose by not trying and that by not succeeding.

Sir Francis Bacon, on
Settling the New World

To be creative, you must take risks.

Leaving the beaten track to wander through the jungle of creativity means leaving the known, flirting with the unknown. In the lives of effective people—especially creative people— risk taking is usually a way of life.

114

But . . . different people choose different risks. Some risk their lives, others gamble with their careers. Some take chances with their psyche; many put their personal self-esteem on the line. Curiously, many who willingly take risks in one way are extremely cautious in other ways. To understand risk taking, you must consider its broad range; physical and financial, intellectual and sexual. A reasonable balance in each area can avoid stagnation.

PHYSICAL RISKS

From time to time—when I feel particularly plugged into the mass-produced life—I

115

like to recall that I am one of the small group
. . . who have seen, and known through their
boot soles, the slopes of Everest. If my sense
of anonymity is especially strong, I concentrate on my membership in an even smaller
fraternity—those of nonmountaineers who
have climbed upon Everest, which makes
me, I suppose, a social climber.

James Lester, psychologist
Psychology Today, 1969

The first and most obvious risk is physical.
People who are avid participants in such activities as motorcycling, skiing, scuba diving,

mountain climbing, parachuting, or auto racing, usually enjoy the others or, at least, are willing to think about doing them. Their limbs are always on the line.

The *benefits* of physical risk taking, when successful, include the thrill of meeting a challenge and succeeding, the camaraderie that grows within a group of daredevils, and the increased self-confidence that comes from knowing you can handle yourself in sticky situations.

The *penalties* of physical risk can be injury, disfigurement, and even death. These penalties should be kept in mind. Taking risks doesn't mean being stupid. As someone once said, "Death is nature's way of telling you to slow down."

Another *penalty* of physical risk taking is the cost. Fast companionship, fast cars, boats, and motorcycles are expensive. Parachuting requires airplanes; scuba diving is best done in clear, tropical waters, usually at resort prices; skiing chews up money like a paper shredder. A common reaction of physical risk takers in the heart of the fray—while careening along in freezing weather on a precariously balanced ice boat, while huddled under the spray of a white-water river raft, while sweating in a fog of dust, burning rubber and gasoline fumes—is, "I paid to be here; this must be fun." As an experienced Sunday sailor wryly put it, "You can create the sensation of an ocean sailing race right at home—put on your shorts, stand under an ice cold shower, and tear up $20 bills while telling yourself how much you are enjoying it."

FINANCIAL RISK

A bright and energetic self-starter can make all the mistakes in this business in five years. With fools and sluggards, it may take a lifetime.

From notes found in an empty
stockbrokers conference room

Financial risk taking is gambling with your money or, more generally, your career, as in changing jobs or taking on expanded responsibilities. In so doing, you are putting your bank account, current and contemplated, on the line.

The *benefit* of financial risk taking, when successful, can be vastly increased financial assets with all the freedom that money can buy, as well as the exhilaration of success in mastering a new system. If the risk includes a successful job change, you will probably enter a new world with wider horizons because such a move inevitably increases your talents and assets, which means you can attempt even larger risks in the future.

The *penalty* of failure is financial loss, perhaps ruin, with the attendant grief and, if the loss continues, a perpetual sense of personal insecurity. A savvy Wall Street reporter, Jerry Goodman, has written a superb book, *The Money Game* (under the pseudonym of Adam Smith) about "image and reality and identity and anxiety and money." In it, he talks about

financial risk taking as a means of establishing an identity but cautions, "If you don't know who you are, the stock market is an expensive place to find out."

INTELLECTUAL RISKS

If you don't take a chance now and then, you stand still—and then you begin to slide backward. [This role] has been almost a new lease on life for me.

Gregory Peck

Intellectual risk taking involves confronting radical new ideas such as political systems, new personal philosophies, changes in life style, or religion—in general, a transformation in your most deeply held beliefs.

The *benefits* of risk taking in the intellectual area include the exhilaration of fresh thinking, the ability to adapt to rapidly changing conditions, and the ability to survive in alien cultures.

The *penalties* of risk taking in the world of ideas—of being wrong—include the pain of inferiority brought by being stupid, and the insecurity that may come from leaving one's traditional values to embrace new beliefs. There is no guarantee that the new philosophy will protect you from future turbulence.

SEXUAL/INTERPERSONAL RISKS

Marriage is the only adventure open to the cowardly.

Voltaire

A fourth type of risk taking is interpersonal or—to take advantage of an alliterative ring with the first three—sexual. Interpersonal risk taking means opening up to another person— telling new acquaintances that you admire them, enjoy being around them, and would like to spend more time with them. This seldom happens in our society, or at least happens very slowly, because we are so afraid of rejection.

The *benefits* of success include expanding your group of friends and intimate acquain-

121

tances, building a social circle for you to share your joys and sorrows with, and perhaps the exhilaration of finding someone else on your wave length. Virginia Woolf vividly described the zing that comes when two new friends meet: "Habits that had seemed durable as stone went down like shadows at the touch of another mind, and left behind a naked sky with fresh stars twinkling in it."

Once you leave your family group, risk taking is the only way that love will come into your life because love always involves danger.

The *penalty* of failure is rejection by others which, for most of us, is one of life's most excruciating experiences. An exchange like:

"Are you free now? Would you like to go for a walk along the river?"

"Gee, I'd like to, but this is the only time I have to do my laundry."

leaves a painful residue that sticks for years. I heard that conversation 25 years ago, and the

searing rejection has only slightly dulled with age. (She eventually married a doctor from Denver—I wonder if she's happy.)

TAKING RISKS GRADUALLY

To live a creative life, one has to gamble, to take some chances, to experiment in at least some of these areas. I believe that the richest life will be lived by those who are taking reasonable risks in all of them.

However, there are risks and then again there are risks—one shouldn't plunge blindly ahead on all fronts, leaving your psyche, physique, and pocketbook exposed to all kinds of failures and penalties.

My personal belief, buttressed by at least some psychological research data, is that you should take risks often when you can afford to lose, but seldom when a failure would be catastrophic.

Risk taking, like most other activities, can be worked up to gradually. Small risks, with small penalties for failure, can be attempted first. If successful, you will increase in both self-confidence and knowledge, and therefore can take on bigger risks. At each point, if you go slowly, you will have a good feeling for where to draw the line which you should not cross because you can no longer afford an unsuccessful outcome.

You can control the outcome of your risks by being prepared and well-informed. To attempt to climb Mt. Everest as an absolute novice would be foolish in the extreme; you would not

123

survive. But to work up to it by studying and practicing climbing techniques, by carefully planning your logistics and strategy, and by joining talented teammates means that your odds will be immeasurably improved. A similar analysis holds in less dramatic settings. The more experienced and better equipped you are, the more likely that your risk will succeed, and that you can continue on to bigger ones with the larger payoffs that come from success. But start slow—in an area where you feel most comfortable. Those areas will expand faster than you might imagine.

Also, you may find that the searing failures that once terrified you no longer seem so catastrophic. The loss of one's job is less threatening after you have successfully changed jobs two or three times and know that it can be done. The loss of a thousand dollars on the stock market is destructive only if it's the last thousand dollars you have. If you have accumulated five or six thousand dollars in the past, however, and know that it can be done again, then the loss of $1000 is placed in a different perspective. The same process operates in the other areas of risk taking as well. Small risks lead to small successes which lead to medium risks which lead to medium successes. Failure will occasionally break the chain, but—if you are cautiously picking your risks—it will only keep you at your current level, not drop you back.

If you want to expand your life, you have to take risks, and as we grow older, that takes more determination. As one of America's most prominent psychologists has said:

> Mature people are apt to learn less than younger people because they are willing to risk less. Learning is a risky business, and we do not like failure. . . . By middle age most of us carry in our heads a tremendous catalogue of things we have no intention of trying again because we tried them once and failed. . . . We pay a heavy price for our fear of failure. It is a powerful obstacle to growth. It assures the progressive narrowing of the personality and prevents exploration and experimentation. There is no learning without some difficulty and fumbling. If you want to keep on learning, you must keep on risking failure—all your life. It's as simple as that.
>
> John Gardner,
> *Self-Renewal*

CHAPTER 10

The Summing Up

I have tried to describe the nature of creativity, the characteristics of creative people, and how you can increase your creative powers. But, as you see by the illustration below, creativity or the creative act is only part of a larger more complicated process that includes three phases.

THE CREATIVE PROCESS

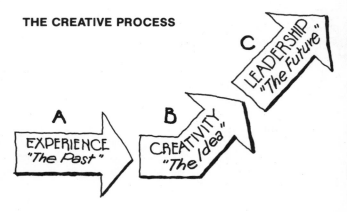

A
EXPERIENCE
"The Past"

B
CREATIVITY
"The Idea"

C
LEADERSHIP
"The Future"

Phase A is the **experience** stage where one picks up the background of the problem—the history, technology, and traditions as well as the inertia that is built into all current programs, problems, and procedures. This stage requires persistence; you have to stay with a problem long enough to thoroughly understand it. An earlier book, *If You Don't Know Where You're Going, You'll Probably End Up Somewhere Else,* dealt with the **experience** phase, specifically with how to collect experiences and assets to have the most possible choices in the future.

Phase B represents the **creativity** phase—the new idea, the change in direction. This phase is usually short in time, but important in impact because it determines a new direction for the future, a direction that will ultimately take on its own history, traditions, and inertia. This phase requires imagination and flexibility, particularly the ability to give up traditional viewpoints and veer off into the new, unexplored directions. This book has dealt with this **creativity** phase.

Phase C represents **leadership**—the new ideas have to be put into practice by verifying them, modifying them, making them work. The ideas that were so exciting on the drawing board now have to be submitted to the hard cold demanding world of reality. The practical concerns of dealing with other people have to be faced here because putting new ideas into practice always involves working through others; new ideas cannot remain hermits. A future third book will deal with the **leadership** phase—how to use your experience and creativity to make things happen through other people.

WHERE IT ALL LEADS

In time the relationship of the three phases— **experience, creativity, leadership**—becomes much more complicated than the first simple diagram would indicate. They become more intimate, and they enrich one another. Finally their relationship is more like the circle below:

Experience leads to the potential for *creativity*, which leads to the possibility of *leadership*, which produces more *experience*, which leads to greater *creativity*, which demands even better *leadership*, which leads to expanding *experiences*, and so forth.

Or, in verse:

> Somewhere there are people who
> Have found creative things to do
> By cultivating skills and new
>   Ideas that softly germinate
>   Then burst in bloom to pollinate
> The thinking of the people who
> Have found creative things to do
> By cultivating skills and new
>   Ideas . . . etc.

Even the circle doesn't capture the full complexity of the process because it is not just one circle. It is a continuum of circles spiraling endlessly upward.

Or, again in verse:

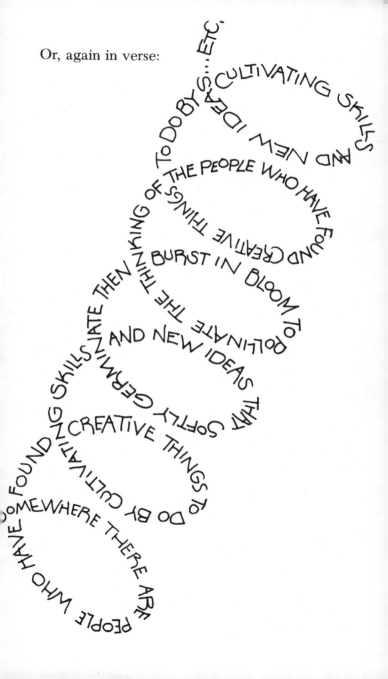

SOMEWHERE THERE ARE PEOPLE WHO HAVE FOUND CREATIVE THINGS TO DO BY CULTIVATING SKILLS AND NEW IDEAS THAT SOFTLY GERMINATE THEN BURST IN BLOOM TO POLLINATE THE THINKING OF THE PEOPLE WHO HAVE FOUND CREATIVE THINGS TO DO BY ... ETC. CULTIVATING SKILLS AND NEW IDEAS

"If you are ever on trial for being creative, what evidence will the prosecutor be able to find?"

Annotated Bibliography

Adams, James L. *Conceptual Blockbusting: A Guide to Better Ideas.* San Francisco: W. H. Freeman, 1974.
A stimulating popular book about expanding your thinking. Well written and fun to read; the book has many useful suggestions.

Barron, Frank. *Creativity and Psychological Health.* Princeton, N.J.: Van Nostand, 1963.
A superb book on creativity written by a psychologist for other psychologists. There is much information here, and a gold mine of philosophic thought in Barron's interpretation of his data from creative people, but the writing is a bit technical for easy reading. Only for seriously motivated students.

Bourke-White, Margaret. *Portrait of Myself.* New York: Simon and Schuster, 1963.
A revealing autobiography by one of the world's best photographers. She discusses her

133

motives, her techniques, her problems and their solutions. Engaging, informative, realistic—a vivid picture of a creative woman.

De Bono, Edward. *Lateral Thinking for Management*. New York: American Management Association, 1971.

An excellent book on the processes of creativity. De Bono discusses the mechanics of creative thinking and uses several puzzles to illustrate his points. He gives many hints and implications for improving the reader's creativity.

Lax, Eric. *On Being Funny: Woody Allen and Comedy*. New York: Manor Books, 1975.

A hilarious book about Woody Allen, writer/comedian/director—one of the world's most creative people. Lax travelled with Allen two years, apparently privy to most of his actions and many of his thoughts. The book is a fine description of what it takes to be outrageously funny, fantastically creative, and astonishingly successful. One of the best books on "applied creativity" that I know.

McLeish, John. *The Ulyssian Adult*. New York: McGraw-Hill, 1976.

A book about creativity in the middle and older years, reassuring for those of us middle-aged and older. The book is a compilation of dramatic creative achievements by "normal" people past the age of 40. A bit ponderous in the writing; still, a fascinating and optimistic account.

Osborn, Alexander F. *Applied Imagination*. New York: Scribner, 1963.

A classic, written by a creative man. Many practical hints on looking at the world differently, on thinking new thoughts, on being imaginative.

Prince, George M. *The Practice of Creativity: A Manual for Dynamic Group Problem Solving.* New York: Harper & Row, 1970.

A useful book about people being creative in small groups. The book focuses on how groups approach problems, on what techniques work best, and on what individuals can do to improve the creativity level of the groups and meetings they are involved in. A well written, helpful book.

Rossman, Joseph. *Industrial Creativity: The Psychology of the Inventor.* Secaucus, N.J.: University Books, 1964.

This book is written by a patent attorney and is mainly about inventors. The author's insights about their motivations are useful. Not for the casual reader.

Watson, James D. *The Double Helix.* New York: Atheneum, 1968.

An informal account of the discovery of DNA by one of the Nobel prize winners involved in the research. The book shares the joys, disappointments, and politics of scientific creativity. It is entertaining and informative for both scientists and laypeople.

Gowan, John C., Demos, G. D. & Torrance, E. P. (eds.), *Creativity: Its Educational Implications.* New York: Wiley & Sons, 1967.

Rothenberg, Albert & Hausman, Carl R. (eds.), *The Creativity Question.* Durham, N.C.: Duke University Press, 1976.

Vernon, Philip (ed.), *Creativity.* New York: Penguin Books, 1970.

These three books are all collections of articles about creativity, usually authored by psychologists. Many of the chapters appear in more than one of these books; all were selected to cover the areas of creativity. These original sources are useful for the serious student of creativity, both for what they contain and for the references they provide to other studies. The range of coverage is extensive. Not recommended for the casual reader.